S0-AYS-046

you're
designed
to shine!

by Christina DiMari

Loveland, Colorado
group.com

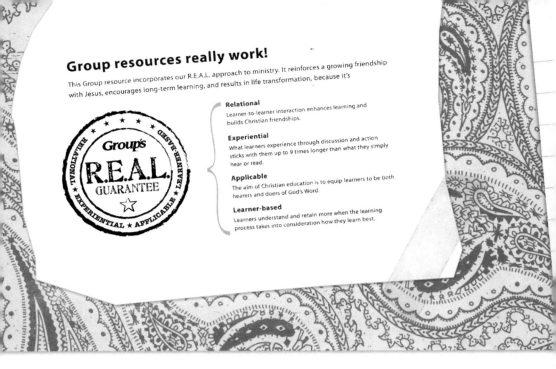

Group resources really work!

This Group resource incorporates our R.E.A.L. approach to ministry. It reinforces a growing friendship with Jesus, encourages long-term learning, and results in life transformation, because it's

Relational
Learner-to-learner interaction enhances learning and builds Christian friendships.

Experiential
What learners experience through discussion and action sticks with them up to 9 times longer than what they simply hear or read.

Applicable
The aim of Christian education is to equip learners to be both hearers and doers of God's Word.

Learner-based
Learners understand and retain more when the learning process takes into consideration how they learn best.

Visit our website: **group.com/women**

This book was written by Christina DiMari, who also provided the photographs you'll see. The editing, design, and other work on this resource were done by the women's ministry team at Group, who love to shine for Jesus!

Unless otherwise indicated, all Scripture quotations are taken from the *Holy Bible*, New Living Translation, copyright © 1996, 2004. Used by permission of Tyndale House Publishers, Inc., Carol Stream, Illinois 60188. All rights reserved.

Some sections of this book have been adapted and reprinted from *Ocean Star*. Copyright © 2006 by Christina DiMari.

Learn more about Christina and her ministry at www.oceanstargifts.com.

ISBN 978-0-7644-7058-5

10 9 8   20 19
Printed in the United States of America.

Thank you!

To all of the Pearls I have met since starting the **You're Designed to Shine!** events. Thank you for using your lives and gifts to shine for others and making knowing and following Jesus attractive. The light is so much brighter because of you!

To Amy Nappa and Group Publishing for "getting" the vision and making this material available to pass on.

To the T-Pod for opening your beach home for our first event and supporting the spread of **You're Designed to Shine!** as it makes its way into girls' lives all over the world.

To Irene Neller, vice president of University Communications and Marketing at Biola University, for being able to see with the eyes of **faith** and joining me on this mission of raising up the next generation of girls to **dream big!**

Table of Contents

Welcome! 6

How to Use *You're Designed to Shine!* 7

Session 1: My Dream 9

Session 2: My Star 21

Session 3: My Pod 33

Session 4: My Pearls 45

Session 5: My Gift 59

Session 6: My Wave 73

Notes for the Leader 87

Welcome!

I'm so excited you've chosen this unique study and interactive experience! During our time together, you'll join with other girls and women on an exciting adventure of discovering that you're designed to shine! You and your girlfriends will be encouraged to:

- explore the dreams you have for your life.
- discover the unique way you shine.
- travel with a supportive pod of friends.
- recognize pearls for your journey.
- learn to exchange gifts with God.
- ride the wave of God's dream for your life.

You don't have to be an ocean girl to be encouraged on our journey together. As you'll soon see, the starfish (or, as I like to call it, ocean star) is a symbol of the amazing truth that we all are stars God has designed to shine. You'll use this book for each session of **You're Designed to Shine!** If you're doing this with a group of friends, you'll each need your own copy, as you'll be writing, drawing, creating, and dreaming on these pages.

So whether you've come from the sea, the mountains, or somewhere in between, it's my hope that you'll enjoy discovering new treasures that will encourage and equip you right now, wherever you are on your journey.

Keep on shining,

Christina DiMari

"The ways of right-living people glow with light; the longer they live, the brighter they shine."
— Proverbs 4:18

How to Use *You're Designed to Shine!*

There are six sessions in *You're Designed to Shine!* Each uses a different symbol from the ocean to represent a Bible-based truth to girls. (And that means "girls" of all ages!) During each session, you will move through a variety of activities that follow this basic flow.

Let's Get Started. This is a welcome, with a Bible verse and the introduction of the topic.

Sharing Stories. This is a portion of Christina's life story that relates to the session. Someone in your group will read this aloud while others follow along in their own books. If you are the leader, be sure to add something personal from your own life so your group has someone right there willing to open her heart and life to them. By sharing *your* story, you're making a connection with the members of your group.

Encouragement. This section includes important words of inspiration and encouragement that many girls rarely (if ever) hear.

Reflections. Here you'll find a series of questions to reflect on and write about.

Create Your Life. This is where you'll write thoughts that you'll later share with others.

Express Yourself. Now you really get to be creative, designing a page that expresses your thoughts, hopes, and dreams. This section uses Scripture, input from others, and your own dreams to tie the session together in a visual way.

Sharing Life. Share your expressions with others. This is a time where you all can open your hearts and hear words of kindness and support from others.

Wrap It Up. You'll draw things to a closing point with final thoughts and prayer.

Closing Thoughts From Christina. This is a section for you to read aloud as a final uplifting word from Christina.

Interwoven into each session, you'll find inspirational thoughts from "Pearls," who are other girls and women from around the world who want to shine for you.

If you're leading *You're Designed to Shine!* you'll find additional tips and helpful notes just for you beginning on page 87.

my dream

"Now all glory to God, who is able, through his mighty power at work within us, to accomplish infinitely more than we might ask or think."
—Ephesians 3:20

"You are God's wonderfully made, loved-beyond-measure daughter. No one can replace you. Go to him to fulfill the desires of your heart, and he will help your dreams come true."
—Allie, a Pearl from California

"A hero is someone who looks up long enough to know there's a better way to go."
—Christina DiMari

" 'For I know the plans I have for you,' says the Lord. 'They are plans for good and not for disaster, to give you a future and a hope.' "
—Jeremiah 29:11

"Each of us is unique, and each of us experiences God in a different way. The art of living is to catch the wave that God wants us to ride and then to ride it passionately—like only you can! He has a special plan for your life, a dream that he only dreams for you.
—Venessa, a Pearl
from South Africa

This session will get you thinking about what you really want to *do* and *be* in life. You may never have thought about what your dream is or the fact that you can *have* a dream. The truth is, there are wide open waters available for you to explore new possibilities and a new life. You'll be able to define your dreams and consider them from God's perspective. Did you even consider that God has a dream for your life?

If you're leading this session, you'll gather art supplies, such as old magazines, markers, pens, colored pencils, scissors, and glue sticks, and place these in a central location.

Let's Get Started!

Open your time together with a brief prayer.

One person from your group can read this aloud:
Wherever you've come from, wherever you find yourself right now, whatever your future holds...you are designed to shine! God has designed you to shine. It doesn't matter your age, your work, or your experience, God has designed you to be unique, like no one else here, and he has a plan for you. Discovering this plan sometimes starts with a simple dream.

The Bible, in Jeremiah 29:11, says, " 'I know the plans I have for you,' says the Lord. 'They are plans for good and not for disaster, to give you a future and a hope.' " Let's replace the word *plans* in this verse with the word *dreams* and read it again.

" 'I know the *dreams* I have for you,' says the Lord. 'They are *dreams* for good and not for disaster, to give you a future and a hope.' "

Today we're going to explore the dreams we have for our lives and consider the dreams God has for our lives, as well.

Every time we meet, we'll share a bit from the life of Christina DiMari, who created *You're Designed to Shine!* Her experiences and reflections are going to be part of our time together.

Choose one person from your group to read the "Sharing Stories" section aloud while everyone else follows along in their own books.

Sharing Stories

When I think of "having a dream," I imagine standing at the edge of the ocean and looking out over the vast blue waters of endless possibilities. I also think of God. He is the giver of all good gifts, including dreams. The first time I realized this, I was in high school.

I grew up in a tumultuous home environment so found my support both in good friends and in the ocean. My friends and I met almost every night at sunset to watch the sun go down over the horizon. We would count from 10 all the way down to 1 as the last specks of light disappeared. It was always a festive time to end the day, knowing we had each other and all was well in our broken worlds.

But there came a time when it all just became too much to handle, and I found myself sitting at the edge of the ocean watching the sunset alone, thinking about what to do with my life. As the sun slipped below the water's edge, I began to lose hope that everything would turn out okay and I could make something better for my future.

As I looked down and closed my eyes, that's when I first heard it. The still, small whisper came to me through the wind and over the waves...**Don't look down at the darkness of the disappearing sun, look up at the color I can paint with your life.** As I lifted my head, I noticed the sun had painted a kaleidoscope of color across the sky. Shades of bright orange, pink, and purple filled the heavens as if an artist had painted a brilliant masterpiece there. The deeper the sun slipped below the water, the brighter the colors glowed in the sky above.

I no longer felt alone. God met me right where I was. And in that amazing moment in time, I realized...God had a dream for my life. I stood up and looked out over the vast blue waters of possibilities and started asking myself this question: What do you want? One by one, I started to articulate the thoughts that came to my mind.

I have heard it said that those who fail to plan, plan to fail. The first step in knowing how to plan is knowing what you want...in other words, what are the dreams you have for your life?

Encouragement

Invite another member of your group to read this aloud:

It's hard to say how a dream starts. It's like a whisper in the back of our mind that keeps telling us we were made for something more. Like a compelling picture in an exciting drama being played out in the realm we can't see, and for a moment, our hearts are captivated that we get to play a significant role in the unfolding story. Through the busyness of our lives, we are wooed by God's calling. *Come. Follow me. Have faith. I have a dream for your life.*

So now is your time to dream. To celebrate your uniqueness and enjoy your life! It's time to move from just thinking about something you'd like to do to actually getting it out of your head and bringing it to reality.

Each of us has a dream that's personal and unique to who we are. As we explore *You're Designed to Shine!* together, we'll discover more tools to help us in this dream. We'll learn more about connecting with the true source of life—God. We'll think about who we "travel" with day to day, we'll uncover "Pearls" we can learn from along the way, gifts we'll receive, all as a part of discovering the big dream God has been dreaming for each of us. For now…let go, have fun, and think big!

What is your dream?

"To write and perform music that touches people, opens their hearts to the Holy Spirit, encourages, blesses, and is relatable to others."

—Jessica, a Pearl from North Carolina

reflections

Read the questions here, and take time to write your thoughts. You'll have the opportunity to share your thoughts later, but now it's time for personal reflection. The quotes you find woven throughout this book are from "Pearls"—young women from around the world who are here to encourage and shine for you as you begin your journey.

Take about 20 minutes for this time of reflection. If you don't finish now, you can do it later.

 What's one thing you'd really like to do in your lifetime?

 Where is one place you'd love to visit?

 How old do you have to be to have a dream? Explain your answer.

 When you were younger, what did you dream about doing or being?

 If you could be like anyone, who would it be?

 If you could create an ideal family, what would it look like?

 If you could have your dream job, what would you do, and where?

 Name three qualities about yourself that make you unique.

 What do you like to do with your free time?

 If you could do one thing to shine for girls coming up the road behind you, what would you do?

create your life

After answering the questions in the "Reflections" section, what's one dream you have for your life right now? Write it in the sand in this picture. Draw a starfish beside your dream. You'll be sharing about this dream with those in your group later.

express yourself!

Have one person read this aloud:

Galatians 6:4-5 says: "Make a careful exploration of who you are and the work you have been given, and then sink yourself into that. Don't be impressed with yourself. Don't compare yourself with others. Each of you must take responsibility for doing the creative best you can with your own life" (from *The Message*).

We're going to use our time now to do just this. We'll explore who we are and take responsibility for doing the creative best we can with our own lives.

On the blank page in this section, illustrate your one big dream with art, pictures, words, stickers, quotes, sand, ribbon, paper, fabric, or anything else that will help you see what your big dream looks like. You may want to use this verse in your expression: *"The Lord says, 'I will guide you along the best pathway for your life. I will advise you and watch over you.' "*—(Psalm 32:8)

When you are done, write a short prayer, and date your page. Wrap it up by looking at your page and defining with one word what it means or says to you. Write that word somewhere on your page.

Shine Bright!

If you need more space for expressing yourself, consider creating a notebook just for your *You're Designed to Shine!* pages. Create and express yourself on larger sheets of paper, and then place these in protective plastic sleeves and keep them as a long-term reminder of your dreams and God's plans for your life.

What is a symbol from nature that is meaningful to you, and what does it remind you of?

"When I look upon the sunset, it is as if I can almost hear God whispering to me, 'I love you.'"

—Faith, a Pearl from California

"The wind. This is something that always causes me to think of God because he appeared to one of the prophets in a whispering wind. All that power, and he chose to show himself in a gentle wind. It makes me reflect on what I think God meant when he says 'Be still and know me.' "

—Amy, a Pearl from Florida

Questions to ponder as you work on your creative page:

Rejoice. What do I have to be thankful for?

Rebuild. How do I struggle with this?

Renew. Look at my life through the eyes of truth. What does the Bible say?

Restore. What is God asking of me to work on? What am I asking of God to do in me?

Refine. What have I learned from this? How will I adjust my life to God's truth?

Remember. What symbol or image will help me remember this?

Role Models. Who shines this truth for me? How?

Ripple. Who can I shine for? How?

Make a Splash!

Make this session even more meaningful with a dried starfish—you can get them at most craft supply stores. If you are at a beach, move to the water's edge and have the group spread out. Use the starfish to write your dreams in the sand in just a few words.

If you're not at a beach, you can pour clean sand into large pans or tubs. Dampen with water ahead of time. Then write your dreams in this sand.

This activity is a great photo opportunity!

Sharing Life

Gather in groups of three or four to share the dream pages you created. This is a time to encourage each other—not a time to laugh at the dreams of another or to discourage someone. Use this time to help a friend dream!

Take at least 10 minutes to share.

Wrap It Up

Gather together, and stand in a circle, holding hands. Have a group member read "Closing Thoughts From Christina" aloud. If you are the leader, share your own closing thoughts so your group time is more personal. Close your time in prayer.

If you're at the beach, do this near the water's edge.

Make a Splash!

Play Jessica McLean's song "Designed to Dream" (from the album by the same name). Jessica's CD can be purchased at www.oceanstargifts.com.

Closing Thoughts From Christina

I get so excited just thinking about the fact that you're starting to look up and realize that God has designed you to dream. There are a few thoughts I want to share with you that have helped me on my journey of defining my dreams and living them out.

After I define what my dream is, the next thing I do is pray. I surrender all my thoughts and dreams to God and actually visualize placing all my dreams before him. Then I ask him to show me if this is something that he would say is good for my life, and I ask him for guidance.

I also like to run my ideas and dreams by a couple of close friends and mentors who I know have my best interests at heart. This is a tricky one. I am always careful to ask for their opinion that is based on their personal knowledge of me. Sometimes when you ask for someone's advice or opinion, they give it based on what **they** would do. They do not have your dream, so be careful to ask them to think about you and your life in this situation.

Next, I start making concrete plans to make my dream a reality. I jot down some short-terms goals that I can start working on now and then some long-term goals that I can work on as the dream takes shape and becomes clearer.

I also funnel the decisions I am faced with through my "dream sifter." This keeps me on task. Each decision you make will help you stay your course and arrive at your destination--or move you off course. The decisions and choices you make are **key** to living out your dreams.

Be flexible. Not very many things go as planned. You'll often need to go with the flow and adjust your course. Dreams can't be rushed or forced or manipulated. They take shape over time and require loads of patience, determination, and faith.

It's a very exciting adventure to dream with God. I pray you will start by looking up and realizing that God desires to paint your life with color!

my star

"Use the gifts and talents that God gave you to bless others and shine bright for God."
— Shannon, a Pearl from Puerto Rico

"Look up into the heavens. Who created all the stars? He brings them out like an army, one after another, calling each by its name. Because of his great power and incomparable strength, not a single one is missing."
— Isaiah 40:26

"Like the starfish, when we connect to God as our Source of Life, we can find healing and restoration in God, thus becoming a whole star, able to shine for others."
— Christina DiMari

"God's promises are true, and his timing is perfect, though sometimes it's easy to forget. It's so important to keep looking up at him and staying connected to his Word. Without a doubt, he loves us and wants the best for us. Sometimes we need to BELIEVE even when we cannot see."
— Elizabeth, a Pearl from California

"My mom died when I was 11 years old. I had some hard times, but I learned to cling to my Rock when the waters got rough. I've learned to be thankful and look to my future, hoping to shine a light for my own family I'm creating now.
— Michele, a Pearl from California

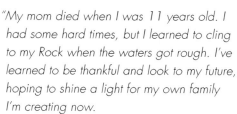

"I have called you by name; you are mine. When you go through deep waters, I will be with you."
— Isaiah 43:1-2

21

starfish is a wonderful reminder of what our lives are like when we have a relationship with Jesus. A starfish can have one of its "arms" cut off—yet as long as it stays in the life source of the ocean, that piece will regrow. When we remain in the life source of Jesus, we can regrow when we are damaged. The starfish clings to a rock to avoid being tossed and battered by the ocean. We can cling to the Rock, Jesus, to avoid being tossed and battered by the world. And the starfish reminds us to shine—shine for Jesus. This session will help you explore these truths, and more!

Supplies and Prep

If you're leading this session, you'll need to gather one starfish for each member of your group. If you used the starfish option in the first session, you can use them again in this session. You'll also need the same art supplies used in Session 1.

Let's Get Started!

Open your time together with a brief prayer.

One person from your group can read this aloud:
Wherever you've come from, wherever you find yourself right now, whatever your future holds...you are designed to shine! God created you to be a unique star that shines unlike anyone else! Let's hear from Christina to learn more about being a shining star. This part of her story involves a few of her friends.

Have one of the group members read the "Sharing Stories" section aloud.

Sharing Stories

I regularly met with my friends Chip, Elena, and others to watch the sun go down over the ocean. One night after we'd celebrated the end of another day, my dog, Ripple, trotted past us with a big starfish flopping from his mouth. We all laughed at the funny sight. It reminded me of a story my dad told me when I was a kid. I told what I could remember to my friends.

"A long time ago, the nighttime sky was filled with bright, shining stars. All we had to do was look up to their light to help us find our way. There were so many zillions of stars to look up to that no one ever got lost. Then one day, some of the stars forgot how to shine for each other.

"One by one, many of them broke and fell from the sky. They landed in the sea. Some people call them starfish, but they're really ocean stars. They're on a journey to learn how to get put back together again. Once they do, they turn back into a star, shining for others the way they were designed to. So if you ever find an ocean star, make sure to be kind and gentle. It's trying to find its way home."

Elena gasped. "Go get the starfish!"

Chip and I almost tripped over a sand castle a few children were building as we chased after Ripple to rescue the ocean star. Taking it out of Ripple's mouth, I brushed off the sand and marveled at the multitude of patterns depicting its life's journey.

"Chip, part of it is broken, but it's still alive," I observed.

"That's what's so cool about a starfish. As long as it's in the ocean, connected to its source of life, it will grow back any piece that gets damaged along the way."

"Wow, that's so amazing!" I said, admiring its intricate design. "If only it were that easy for us. We'd just live the rest of our life in the water."

"Not a bad idea," Chip said with a chuckle.

"Hurry, throw it back in the ocean!" Elena hollered, catching up to us. I clutched it in my hand like a Frisbee and flung it as hard as I could, sending the ocean star back to sea.

Encouragement

Give each girl an ocean star (starfish). Invite one person to read the following aloud while others follow along in their own books:

During this session, we're going to explore what it means to become a star that shines brightly. Throughout *You're Designed to Shine!* we'll examine a variety of symbols related to the ocean that can help us understand our relationship with Jesus and others. The starfish is the symbol we're going to explore in this session.

We're going to move to our time of reflection. Look at your starfish. Read about this amazing creature God created. See what you can learn for your own life as you compare this star to your life and the lessons God is teaching you.

Read the questions here, and take time to write your thoughts. You'll have the opportunity to share your thoughts later, but now it's time for personal reflection. Take about 20 minutes for this time of reflection. If you don't finish now, you can do it later.

The ocean star shows us many truths about our lives and our relationship with God. Take time to look at your own ocean star, and then write your thoughts about these different ways the ocean star can be a symbol to us.

 ## Look Up

When you look up at the stars, what do you think about? God says he knows the stars and calls them each by name. How does that make you feel?
Do you believe you are more valuable or unique than a star?
Why or why not?

"Look up into the heavens. Who created all the stars? He brings them out like an army, one after another, calling each by its name."
—Isaiah 40:26

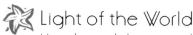

Light of the World

How do stars help us or guide us? The Bible refers to Jesus as the Bright Morning Star. Why would that be good news to you?

"I am the bright morning star."
—Revelation 22:16

Get Connected

A starfish can be healed from injuries—even as severe as losing a limb—if it stays in the life source of the ocean. When it stays in the ocean, it also avoids drying up and dying. When you think about connecting to God as your Source of Life, where are you on that journey?

When looking at your star, are there any pieces that look injured or even cut off? How would you compare this with your own life? Where do you long for God's healing?

"God made my life complete when I placed all the pieces before him."
—Psalm 18:20, *The Message*

Believe

Look on the "arms" of your starfish for a tiny orange "eyespot." The starfish cannot see but navigates its way by its keen sense of light and dark. How is that like or unlike your journey of faith?

"Your word is a lamp to guide my feet and a light for my path."
—Psalm 119:105

Hold on Tight

When out in the tumbling waves, the starfish holds on tightly to rocks to avoid being tossed up on shore or dashed against other objects. When the waves of life threaten to toss you around, what do you hold on to? What or who is your rock? How do you hold on tightly?

"He alone is my rock and my salvation, my fortress where I will never be shaken."
—Psalm 62:2

 Shine Bright

When Jesus, the Bright Morning Star, is at the center of your star, how does that help you shine? Who can you shine the light of Jesus upon today? How will you do this?

"Those who are wise will shine as bright as the sky, and those who lead many to righteousness will shine like the stars forever."
—Daniel 12:3

create your life

Kind

"I'd say you'll do best by filling your minds and meditating on things true, noble, reputable, authentic, compelling, gracious—the best, not the worst; the beautiful, not the ugly; things to praise, not things to curse. Put into practice what you learned from me, what you heard and saw and realized. Do that, and God, who makes everything work together, will work you into his most excellent harmonies."
(Philippians 4:8-9, *The Message*)

Generous

My Rock

Follow Jesus

Love

Shine Bright

Dream

Dive Deep

Connect

Courage

Peace

Good

Circle the word on this page that best shows where you are on your journey right now as it relates to what you've discovered through your time of reflection. Then write down all the things you want to bring into your life today that will help your star shine bright.

Take about 5 minutes for this.

Faithful

Express Yourself

Have one person read this aloud:

Isaiah 40:26-27 says: "Look up into the heavens. Who created all the stars? He brings them out like an army, one after another, calling each by its name. Because of his great power and incomparable strength, not a single one is missing."

Right now we're going to take time to creatively express what God is teaching us about being shining stars. Consider what it means to shine for God. What does it mean to shine into the life of someone else?

Use the blank page in this section to express yourself as it relates to shining as a star. Draw a picture of yourself (a stick figure is OK!) in relation to where you are now and where you want to be. Be creative…draw the ocean, sand, shore, water, waves, and your "ocean star." What picture best describes where you are on your journey of connecting to God as your Source of Life right now? What picture best describes where you want to be? Choose a verse from the "Reflections" page to include with your expression.

You'll see questions to ponder as you work. You'll see quotes from girls who have gone before you. You can use any of the art supplies gathered here or anything else you find that will help you express your dream. You'll have about 20 minutes.

When you are done, write a short prayer, and date your page.

Questions to ponder as you work on your creative page:

Rejoice. What do I have to be thankful for?

Rebuild. How do I struggle with this?

Renew. Look at my life through the eyes of truth. What does the Bible say?

Restore. What is God asking of me to work on? What am I asking of God to do in me?

Refine. What have I learned from this? How will I adjust my life to God's truth?

Remember. What symbol or image will help me remember this?

Role Models. Who shines this truth for me? How?

Ripple. Who can I shine for? How?

What's one thing you have overcome?

"Maybe being the center of attention? 'Social butterfly,' that was me! Didn't miss a party or a chance to win favor with others. After coming to know Christ, I now crave only HIS attention. And in knowing I have HIS attention, I have learned that he has a wave for me to ride and a dream to fulfill while I am on this earth. I now spend my time shining for others to see HIM."

—Lisa, a Pearl from Barbados

What do you want to say to girls working on this page?

"You have to go through the fire to be refined, but you come out shining brighter than before. The journey never ends, but you are never alone."

—Wendy, a Pearl from the Netherlands

Sharing Life

Gather in groups of three or four to share the star pages you created. This is a time to encourage each other—not a time to laugh at the dreams of another or to discourage someone. Use this time to shine encouragement into the life of a friend!

Take at least 10 minutes to share.

Wrap It Up

Gather together, and stand in a circle, holding hands. Have a group member read the "Closing Thoughts From Christina" aloud. If you are the leader, share your own closing thoughts so your group time is more personal. Close your time in prayer.

Closing Thoughts From Christina

No matter where you are on your journey right now, I want you to know that God will meet you right where you are. Whether you are on the shore looking out at the water, just starting to get your star connected to the tide, or down deep exploring new depths of God's grace....know that you are loved.

For those of you who have ever felt lost, look up—the Bright Morning Star is shining for you, showing you how to find your way home. For those of you who have ever felt broken, bruised, or hurt along your journey, I understand. The good news is, God has sent his Son into this world to mend your broken heart. He did it for me. He can do it for you, too. Continue to read his words; they will soothe your soul. If you ever feel unsure of which way to go, his words will throw a beam of light onto your path.

Stay in tune with God's leading and working in your life. Have faith. Be brave. Stay pure. When the waves of life threaten to toss you about, find the Rock and hold on tight!

And ultimately, remember, you were not designed to be broken. You were designed to shine! When Christ is invited to be the center of your star, he will fill you up with light and shine through your lives to be a light in the world. And our world needs that light. So wherever you found yourself in this session, I encourage you to consider taking the next step closer or deeper...no one or no thing will ever satisfy you the way Jesus can. Go ahead—dive deep and explore anew what God has to say about love and life and his purpose for your star!

Make a Splash!

Play Jessica McLean's song "Designed to Dream."

my pod

"Show me your friends, and I'll show you your future! There are people in our lives who lift us up, keep us afloat, and encourage us. Buoys. Then there are people who drain us, tear us down, and take our energy. Anchors. Most of us have both of these kinds of people in our lives. I have learned over the years to surround myself with more buoys and fewer anchors."

—Diana, a Pearl from California

"If one person falls, the other can reach out and help. But someone who falls alone is in real trouble."

—Ecclesiastes 4:10

"When I am at the beach and see dolphins swimming by the shore, I feel like God is revealing something special to me. I love to sit and wait and watch for dolphins and talk to God when I'm at the beach."

—Claire, a Pearl from California

"There is no greater love than to lay down one's life for one's friends."

—John 15:13, The Message

"My pod consists of the most amazing, godly, and inspiring best friends I have ever had. What makes this pod so special is that it reflects the very type of relationship that God intended for human beings to experience because it gathers its strength from the author of friendship, God Himself. What a blessing it is to know that no matter what, I can rely on my friends to challenge, encourage, support, and nurture me on my path to living a life that truly resembles that of Jesus Christ."

—Faith, a Pearl from California

This session focuses on the importance of friendship and choosing friends wisely. Friendship is important, but "friends" who tear you down instead of lift you up aren't really friends at all. Encourage each other to consider who you're choosing as friends, what kind of friend you are yourself, and how to be more like dolphins who travel together, support each other, and protect each other.

Supplies and Prep

If you're leading this session, you'll need to gather art supplies, such as old magazines, markers, pens, colored pencils, scissors, and glue sticks, and place these in a central location.

Let's Get Started!

Open your time together with a brief prayer.

One person from your group can read this aloud:
Wherever you've come from, wherever you find yourself right now, whatever your future holds…you are designed to shine! But it's really hard to shine if you're being crushed, torn apart, or discouraged by so-called friends—or if you're not being the kind of friend God meant you to be. Today we'll look to the ocean for a lesson about friendship. But first, let's hear a part of Christina's story.

Have someone read the "Sharing Stories" section aloud.

Sharing Stories

I was at the beach with my dog, Ripple, and my friends Katie and Elena, ready to watch the sunset. As the sun was about to drop below the horizon, the four of us stood at the water's edge and let the rising tide wash over our bare feet. By our side, Ripple dug furiously for sand crabs.

Elena interrupted our contemplation. "Look! There's a dolphin pod in the roll wave down shore!" We ran down the beach until we could see them clearly.

"Wow! I've never seen a dolphin pod in real life!" Katie exclaimed.

"Me neither," I admitted.

We stood side by side and relished the joy of watching the pod effortlessly surf the roll wave. Elena broke into a wolf howl, hoping to connect with the dialect of the dolphins. We all bent over laughing. Then we listened.

There was magic in the air. Something we'd never experienced was happening between the dolphin pod and us. The quieter we became, the more we felt it. The dolphins knew something that we needed to know. I wanted to know what it was.

Beyond the expanse of what I knew my world to be, I looked at the dolphin pod and saw its symbol of hope.

"That's it!" I exclaimed. "We'll be like a dolphin pod. We'll travel together like they do. And we can protect each other from all the sharks that want to tear us apart."

It was clear that my friends understood what I had seen in the dolphins.

"I read that when one dolphin in a pod is injured, two healthy dolphins immediately come to help. They swim under the dolphin in trouble and support her with their flippers. Then they bring the dolphin to the surface so she can catch her breath," Katie added excitedly. "They help each other when times are tough."

"It's like they have a strong connection with each other," Elena said. "They know how to be friends—just like we do."

"Yeah, they don't leave each other when the going gets tough," I said. "Instead, they show up for each other!"

Encouragement

Have another member of your group read this aloud:

We can't go through life alone. We need friends to travel beside us, lift us up at times, offer words of encouragement, and enjoy the journey with us as we live out God's dreams for our lives. But we see so many negative examples all around us. Friends that aren't friends at all. People who tear each other down, gossip about each other, and who hurt us over and over. We don't want to have friends like this, and we don't want to *be* friends like this.

We can learn so many great lessons about friendship from dolphins. On the following pages, we'll find interesting facts about dolphins, along with questions for us to reflect on and write about. Let's take time to do that now.

Read the following facts, and reflect on the questions. Write your thoughts. You'll have about 20 minutes to do this. It's OK to talk to each other, but remember to use your own reflections instead of the ideas of others.

Dolphins can choose different dolphins to travel with—they can stay with one pod for a while and then move to a new pod.

- List at least five qualities you look for in a friend. How important are these qualities? Have you found friends that have these qualities?

- What kind of friend are you? List at least five qualities that describe what kind of friend you are.

- How could you improve as a friend? List two areas you want to improve in.

Dolphins can be observed playing, and scientists think that dolphins like to have fun.

- What do you think you can learn from dolphins?
- What are ways to have fun that are both safe and honoring to God?

 Dolphins support each other. When one dolphin in a pod is injured, two healthy dolphins will put their fins under the dolphin who has been injured and bring it up to the surface where it can breathe. They hold it there until it is able to be on its own.

- How are you doing this for your friends?
- How are your friends doing this for you? What are specific examples?
- Is God in your pod? If so, how do you count on him? How is God supportive of you?

Dolphins join together and circle around to protect each other (and sometimes even humans!) from sharks.

- Who are the sharks (people you don't feel safe or comfortable with) that you want to keep outside of your circle?
- How can your friends circle around and protect you from these people?
- What do you do when a friend you thought was a dolphin starts acting like a shark?

Beside each of the dolphins in this picture, write the names of people who are currently in your "pod." These people might be family, friends, neighbors, mentors, and so on. Under each name write something you like about that person.

At the outer edge of this page, write the names of the sharks you want to keep outside of your inner circle.

Take about 5 minutes to do this.

Who is in your dolphin pod, and how do you support each other?

"I try to surround myself with friends who are living lives that glorify God and who purpose in their hearts to obey God. We do things together that are fun and beneficial, rather than things that are potentially harmful to ourselves or to others. We try to be honest with each other and talk openly about our struggles and triumphs."

—Becky, a Pearl from Hawaii

"To have healthy friendships, it's important to stay in touch, even if you live apart, and to care about what is going on in each other's lives."
—Sadie, a Pearl from Tennessee

"A healthy friendship doesn't mean you are constantly with that person or tell them your every thought. Sometimes the healthiest friendships give each other space and don't try to make that person complete you. Instead, we support and encourage each other."
—Macie, a Pearl from Alabama

"My husband and kids and my many friends that I talk to regularly, who are shaping who I am, teaching about the goodness of God, and loving me deeply in grace and truth."

—Nancy Ortberg,
a Christian author
from California

Express Yourself

Have one person read this aloud:

Ecclesiastes 4:10 gives us a reason to travel with a pod. It says, "If one person falls, the other can reach out and help. But someone who falls alone is in real trouble." We're going to use our time now to explore our friendships and express how we see our pod right now—or perhaps how we'd like it to look.

On the blank page in this section, express yourself with a visual image of your pod. Use pictures, words, stickers, quotes, sand, ribbon, paper, fabric, or anything else that will help you see what your pod looks like. This will help you as you interact in your current relationships and as you choose new people to be in your pod.

You may want to use this verse in your expression: *"If one person falls, the other can reach out and help. But someone who falls alone is in real trouble"* (Ecclesiastes 4:10).

You'll have about 20 minutes. When you are done, write a short prayer and date your page.

Questions to ponder as you work on your creative page:

Rejoice. What do I have to be thankful for?

Rebuild. How do I struggle with this?

Renew. Look at my life through the eyes of truth. What does the Bible say?

Restore. What is God asking of me to work on? What am I asking of God to do in me?

Refine. What have I learned from this? How will I adjust my life to God's truth?

Remember. What symbol or image will help me remember this?

Role Models. Who shines this truth for me? How?

Ripple. Who can I shine for? How?

Sharing Life

Gather in groups of three or four to share the pod pages you created. This is a time to encourage each other—not a time to laugh at the dreams of another or to discourage someone. It's the time to really be a dolphin and not a shark!

Take at least 10 minutes to share.

Wrap It Up

Gather together, and stand in a circle, holding hands. Have a group member read the "Closing Thoughts From Christina" aloud. If you are the leader, share your own closing thoughts so your group time is more personal. Close your time in prayer.

If you're at the beach, do this near the water's edge.

Closing Thoughts From Christina

I hope you had a fun time today looking at the pod of people you're traveling through life with. This was an important thing for me to do because I wasn't as blessed as some of you who have amazing parents and families. As I've gotten older, now my husband and my own children are also in my pod. I have had people that wanted to travel with me in my pod, but they were not healthy for me, and I had to keep them outside my inner circle. For the most part, **you** get to choose who you travel with.

Take a good look at the people in your pod, and make sure they're people who are healthy for you and you for them. If you're around people who pull you down because they struggle with jealousy, manipulation, anger, resentment, bitterness, lying, and activities you don't want to be a part of, realize in most situations **you** can change this. It's up to you with whom you choose to keep company.

I want you going toward your dreams. I want you going toward more opportunities where your light will shine. Keep those near you who will support you. Look for friends who rejoice with you when you succeed. Look for friends who reflect qualities like joy, peace, contentment, love, and courage. Life is short—don't waste time following people down dead-end roads. Travel with others who desire Christ to be the center of their lives. And then encourage each other to stay true to who you are and use your gifts to shine for others in creative and unique ways.

Make a Splash!

Play Jessica McLean's song "Designed to Dream."

my pearls

"Let us think of ways to motivate one another to acts of love and good works."
—Hebrews 10:24

"Each pearl on your strand represents someone who has been a Pearl to you in some way along your journey. Because they crossed your path, you have been encouraged to fly, pursue your dreams, and reach your highest potential."
—Christina DiMari

Who is a Pearl to you?

"My mother-in-law, Linda, has shown me that a woman's strength, dignity, and power come from her faith in God."
—Jennifer Strickland, an international model, author, and Pearl from Texas

"For the Lord God is our sun and our shield. He gives us grace and glory. The Lord will withhold no good thing from those who do what is right."
—Psalm 84:11

This session is all about women being transformed into a beautiful Pearl. A Pearl is a girl or woman who started out as a simple grain of sand, and through the irritations she encountered on her journey, she allowed God to refine and mold her into something beautiful. She now allows God to be the center of her life and desires his love, grace, and glory to shine through her in creative ways to be a light for others. As Pearls shine, they have a ripple effect on the lives of others around them, becoming mentors who add value and inspiration.

Today you'll consider how you can shine for others—and how you can find women who will shine into your life, as well.

Supplies and Prep

If you're leading this session, you'll need a pearl or strand of pearls for each person. You might want to put these into a shell or other creative container until you're ready to use them. You can use inexpensive freshwater pearls if you like.

You'll also need the same art supplies as in previous sessions.

Let's Get Started!

Open your time together with a brief prayer. Then have one person from your group read this aloud:

Wherever you've come from, wherever you find yourself right now, whatever your future holds…you're designed to shine! Discovering how to shine often depends on the example of others—Christina calls these women "Pearls"—who will encourage us along the way. Let's find out how Christina found a Pearl to help guide her.

Have someone read "Sharing Stories" aloud.

Sharing Stories

A little girl had dime-store pearls she cherished more than anything else. One day her father asked her to give him the pearls. Over and over again she said, "No, you can take anything but the pearls." All along, the girl's father had a beautiful strand of genuine pearls in his pocket to give her in exchange for her dime-store set. The moral of the story is that when we are asked to surrender something, it often is because God has plans to replace it with something much better.

I was going through a season in my life when I wished I had an older friend to talk to who might be able to understand what I was feeling. As always, when I feel this way, I turn to God and talk to him about everything I am feeling and then ask him to speak to me through his Word.

I came across this verse: "The Lord God is a sun and shield; the Lord will give grace and glory; no good thing will He withhold from those who walk uprightly" (Psalm 84:11, NKJV).

In my prayer journal, I began to illustrate what this verse meant to me in relation to how God would provide what I was looking for. I drew a sun, illustrated like a shining pearl, to became my symbol of how God would provide for me with his companionship, understanding, and comfort; a purple shield was my symbol of how God would provide for me through the guidance of his Word. The symbols represented that I belonged to him—I was his child.

That's how we shine! When we allow God's blessing to be the center of our lives, our value and worth and ability to shine come not from others but from God making his home inside of us.

In my prayer time, I surrendered a dime-store strand of pearls that my grandmother gave me as a child and asked God to help me look to him for all my needs. For two years I studied everything I could about the lessons in Psalm 84:11. How God is a Sun. A Shield. Grace. Glory. Good things. Walking uprightly.

I was surprised one day as I opened the front door and saw a present someone had dropped off for my birthday. It was snowing. A strong sensation surrounded me that God had something to do with this present. Deep in my heart I heard him whisper, **This is from me.** I put the gift on my lap. Time seemed to stand still as I reached inside the box.

I lifted out a small blue satin pouch, unzipped the top, and pulled out the most beautiful, unique set of freshwater pearls I'd ever seen. Tears welled up in my eyes. Only God could have known about the fake pearls I surrendered.

I ran my fingers gently over each pearl, feeling its unique shape. Looking closer, I let out a shout. "There's a sun and a shield!" On the outside of the clasp was one solitary pearl shaped like the sun and one purple stone shaped like a shield, the exact symbols I had drawn in my art journal!

Then, in the deep places in my heart, God began to reveal the meaning of my gift:
Continue to look to me for all of your needs. I am your Sun, your Shield, your Source of Life. By continually looking up, you have allowed me to take the irritations of your life and mold you into a beautiful pearl. It is time now for you to take what you have learned and pass it on to girls coming up the road behind you.

Each pearl on your strand represents someone who has been a Pearl to you in some way along your journey. Because they crossed your path, you have been encouraged to fly, pursue your dreams, and reach your highest potential. They spoke words that lit your path, walked with you awhile, or cheered from afar. Authors motivated you, music moved you, and unexpected strangers inspired you. Think about the people who have added value to your life. These are your Pearls. These people have passed a blessing on to you. The lessons you have learned from them are like a strand of pearls around your neck as you continue your journey of becoming the beautiful Pearl God is designing you to be. A unique young woman who not only follows her own dreams but is willing to take time to shine for others, as well.

Encouragement

Have another member of your group read this aloud:

So far on our journey together, we've had a dream, we've learned about being like a star, and we're traveling with a supportive pod of people. Now we're going to consider the people God's put in our lives to encourage us along the way. We'll call these people "Pearls." Not only will God put Pearls in your life, *you* are going to be a Pearl for many, too!

When a simple grain of sand enters into the living membrane of an oyster, it causes the oyster fits of irritation. The oyster's reaction is to coat that grain of sand with a substance called *nacre*. Over time, the layers of nacre build up and become a pearl.

We are like the grain of sand when we come to God. He takes us as we are, and through the irritations we encounter on our journey, he coats us with his grace, refines us, and molds us into something of beauty that reflects his love to the world. We are Pearls when we realize our great value is Christ in us, shining through our lives.

reflections

A Pearl is someone who has spoken value into your life, encouraged you to pursue your dreams, and helped you reach your highest potential. A Pearl shines for you somehow in your relationship with God, speaks words that light your path, walks with you awhile, or cheers from afar. A Pearl could be a family member, a friend, a neighbor, or the author of a book you read. It could a stranger you met, who had no idea she impacted your life.

Six characteristics to look for in a Pearl:

- Someone who taps into what God is doing in you
- Someone who is an encourager
- Someone who covers you with prayer
- Someone who demonstrates understanding
- Someone who shows love
- Someone with patience

Six characteristics to avoid:

- Someone who wants to force her ideas on you
- Someone who uses you for her own personal gain
- Someone who insists that she is always right
- Someone who uses manipulative words and actions
- Someone with a critical spirit
- Someone who has an unhealthy emotional connection

Read the questions here, and take time to write your thoughts. You'll have the opportunity to share your thoughts later, but now it's time for personal reflection. Take about 20 minutes for this time of reflection. If you don't finish now, you can do it later.

 Who has shone a light for you on your journey of becoming who you are today?

 What teacher added value to who you are today?

 What author has given you guidance?

 What relative, neighbor, or person in your community is a role model for you in some way?

 How does God shine for you and guide you?

 How can you be a Pearl and shine for others who are coming up the road behind you?

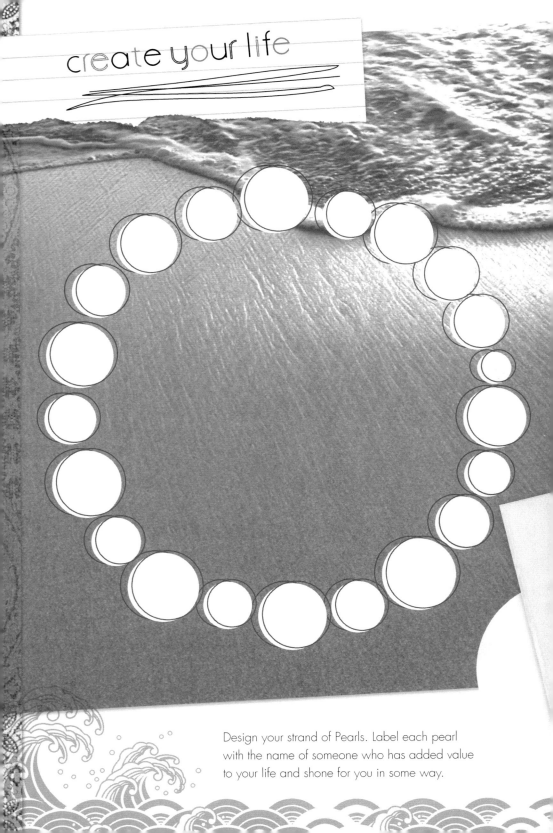

create your life

Design your strand of Pearls. Label each pearl
with the name of someone who has added value
to your life and shone for you in some way.

Who has been a Pearl to you, and how?

"'Do I just need to be fixed?' I felt like there was something wrong with me. How come I could love Jesus but turn away from him in a moment when guys came around? Their attention seemed more important than his. I hated myself for this. I opened his Word to Hosea 14:4: 'I will heal their waywardness and love them freely....' The word 'heal' caught my attention... God didn't see me as a problem to be 'fixed' but his daughter who needed healing! I asked God to heal the wounds deep inside from sexual abuse and rejection, and he HEALED my waywardness!"

—Olivia, a Pearl from Florida

"Pearls to me symbolize God's infinite grace. A pearl is formed when an intruder such as a grain of sand or any irritating substance goes inside the oyster. The oyster then coats the intruder as a way to protect itself from the foreign substance. God has coated me with his grace. All the people who have extended grace and love to me are my Pearls."

—Ana, a Pearl from Rhode Island

Express Yourself

Have one person read this aloud:

Hebrews 10:24 says, "Let us think of ways to motivate one another to acts of love and good works." This verse reminds us how important it is to be encouraging to others—and how important it is to have others around who will encourage us. We're going to use our creativity now to show who our Pearls are or who we hope to become Pearls for.

On the blank page in this section, express how one or more of your Pearls impacted your life. Do you remember the words they spoke to you? A quote from a book? A Bible verse that has thrown a beam of light on your path? What value has each Pearl added to you? What have you learned that you want to remember?

Use pictures, words, stickers, quotes, sand, ribbon, paper, fabric, or anything else that will help you see what your Pearls look like. You may want to use this verse in your expression: "*Let us think of ways to motivate one another to acts of love and good works*" (Hebrews 10:24).

When you are done, write a short prayer, and date your page.

Questions to ponder as you work on your creative page:

Rejoice. What do I have to be thankful for?

Rebuild. How do I struggle with this?

Renew. Look at my life through the eyes of truth. What does the Bible say?

Restore. What is God asking of me to work on? What am I asking of God to do in me?

Refine. What have I learned from this? How will I adjust my life to God's truth?

Remember. What symbol or image will help me remember this?

Role Models. Who shines this truth for me? How?

Ripple. Who can I shine for? How?

Sharing Life

Gather in groups of three or four to share the Pearls pages you created. Remember to make this a time of encouragement.

Take at least 10 minutes to share.

Wrap It Up

Now is the time for each group member to receive her own pearl to keep. The leader can let each person pick out her own pearl from the container, for extra meaning. As each one takes a pearl, invite others in the group to say words of encouragement to her, affirming her as one of God's Pearls.

Then gather together, and stand in a circle, holding hands. Have a group member read the "Closing Thoughts From Christina" aloud. If you are the leader, share your own closing thoughts so your group time is more personal. Close your time in prayer.

If you're at the beach, do this near the water's edge.

Closing Thoughts From Christina

As you continue your journey of pursuing your dreams, becoming the shining star God designed you to be, and traveling with a supportive pod of friends, I pray that God will surround you with many pearls along the way. Keep your eyes open. God loves to surprise you! Your next pearl may be the author of a book you read. The musician of the next song that speaks truth into your life. The random person you struck up a conversation with on your walk down the beach, along a mountain stream, or down the path by your house. It may be the pastor in your church, a teacher in your school, or the clerk at the store. Remember, no two pearls are alike. Not one pearl is perfect. Enjoy each pearl for who they are, and appreciate the value they have passed on to your life.

As you hold your pearl in your hand, remember that God has his eye on you. There may be times when you feel like the grain of sand inside the oyster. No matter what irritations you encounter on this earth, you know now that if you bring them to God, he will coat you with his grace and shape you into a beautiful pearl. The lessons you learned along the way will become new ways that you will shine for others.

Now, think about the girls and women coming up the road behind you. How can you be a pearl for them? Can you think of one that you can be a pearl for this week? Be sure to pray for that person today.

Make a Splash!

Play Jessica McLean's song "Designed to Dream."

my gift

"Whatever is good and perfect comes down to us from God our Father, who created all the lights in the heavens. He never changes or casts a shifting shadow."
—James 1:17

"Now all glory to God, who is able, through his mighty power at work within us, to accomplish infinitely more than we might ask or think."
—Ephesians 3:20

"I am very blessed to have grown up in a Christian home. It was probably the beginning of high school when I took my faith as my own. I had believed in Christ for so long, but now I needed to surrender and give God every area of my life."
—Savannah, a Pearl from Texas

"Sometimes we need to let go before God can take us to the place we need to be. After all, everything we have comes from the Lord, so we're only giving back what was once first given to us."
—Andrea, a Pearl from Virginia

"And may the Lord make your love for one another and for all people grow and overflow, just as our love for you overflows."
—1 Thessalonians 3:12

ertainly all of us have wondered at one time or another, What does God want from me? What can I give him? What do I have that God could use? This session will help you consider both what God is reaching out to offer you and what you can offer God through your life. It will become a gift exchange, with each person accepting what God has for her life and offering a gift of surrender to God.

Supplies and Prep

If you're leading this session, you'll need to gather art supplies, such as old magazines, markers, pens, colored pencils, scissors, and glue sticks, and place these in a central location.

For this session, you'll also need:

- 1 small gift box per person—choose a pretty gold-foil box if at all possible. This is to represent a special gift!

- pink curling ribbon

- sheets of blank paper; pens or pencils

Let's Get Started!

Open your time together with a brief prayer. Then have one person from your group read this aloud:

Wherever you've come from, wherever you find yourself right now, whatever your future holds…you are designed to shine! Shining that light often depends on surrendering things you think are important so that you can receive something God knows is much better for you in the long run. Let's hear from Christina for her story as it relates to this.

Have someone read "Sharing Stories" aloud.

Sharing Stories

When I was a young girl growing up near the beach, I used to write notes to God and then stuff each one inside a balloon, blow it up, and let it go. I'd tilt my head back, watching the balloon get smaller and smaller until it disappeared into the sky far above me. Then I wondered. Did God get my message? Did he hear me? Will he answer me?

You may not have put a message in a balloon, but I'm sure you've experienced times in your own life when you wondered if God heard you and if he would somehow let you know. And I'm sure you've wondered what he wants from you in your life.

Once, when I asked God, "What do you want from me?" I felt this whisper in my heart, "I want your will." I was going through a time in my life when I was holding onto control, and God was wooing me to let go and let **him** be in control.

I thought about it for awhile, and then I went downstairs where my boys had a box full of play horses. I cut off the reins of one of the white horses and put this inside a small gift box. I was like, "Here, God...I let go...I surrender...you can have the reins of my life."

A couple days later I received a note in the mail from a friend. The whole front of the card was a picture of a white horse running playfully through crystal blue water, with the rider holding onto the reins. I was stunned. It was God's way of telling me...I got it. Not only that, the horse and rider were in the most beautiful water I had ever seen, and the rider was full of excitement for this adventure he seemed to be embarking on. This expressed to me that God had my reins now, and I had better hold on!

Then I was reading in my Bible and came across Revelation 19:11, which says, "Then I saw heaven opened, and a white horse was standing there. Its rider was named Faithful and True, for he judges fairly and wages a righteous war."

God was beginning to teach me that he could be trusted with my heart and life because he is Faithful and True. I spent several months studying what it meant to be faithful and true. A simple act of surrender opened up a whole new way for me to get to know the heart of my God I was still learning how to trust.

Encouragement

Have another person in your group read this aloud:

Most of us think of the word *surrender* as it relates to war. We picture someone coming out with his or her hands raised, saying, "I give up! I surrender!" But surrender can also relate to giving someone else power or control of our lives or even of specific situations in our lives.

Our time today is all about surrendering something in our own lives to God. What can we give him? We're certain to learn something new and grow in our friendship with Jesus as we give him more and more of our lives. We're going to think of this as a gift exchange, where we accept any gift we believe is from God and offer him the gift of surrendering a part of our lives.

As you begin to think about what *surrender* means in your relationship with God, reflect on these steps as we read them aloud.

Take turns reading each of the following sections aloud.

 ## Communication

Talk to God...about everything. Then listen. That's the fun part. The way he answers is almost always different from anything you may anticipate. He loves to surprise you. He longs to make himself known. He goes to great lengths to reveal himself. Your part? Look around you. Signs of his presence are everywhere!

 ## Trust

For those of you who have experienced betrayal, it may be hard for you to trust anyone, even God. But God doesn't play games with you. He's not shifty or manipulative. He has your best interests at heart...always.

Surrender

As we give God control, he can clear out what we don't need to make room for what he'd designed for us all along.

Acceptance

After surrender comes a season where we're led to accept being content with or without whatever we surrendered. This involves being at peace with trusting God's best for our lives.

Creation

During this time, God may mold our hearts, change our attitudes, or renew our minds. At other times, he creates something totally new in our lives, something above and beyond anything we could ever ask or imagine. He knows the gifts he put within us that are still waiting to be unwrapped. His desire is to provide all we need to live to our full potential of making him known in this world.

Symbols

During or after this process of surrender, consider a symbol that will remind you of what God is doing in your life. These objects or images are helpful in keeping our minds focused on what God has spoken in our hearts and lives.

reflections

Consider these verses and what they mean to your life. Write your thoughts.

"The Lord will withhold no good thing from those who do what is right."
—Psalm 84:11

"Take delight in the Lord, and he will give you your heart's desires."
—Psalm 37:4

"And may you have the power to understand, as all God's people should, how wide, how long, how high, and how deep his love is. May you experience the love of Christ, though it is too great to understand fully. Then you will be made complete with all the fullness of life and power that comes from God."
—Ephesians 3:18-19

"Whatever is good and perfect comes down to us from God our Father, who created all the lights in the heavens. He never changes or casts a shifting shadow."
—James 1:17

"How precious are your thoughts about me, O God. They cannot be numbered! I can't even count them; they outnumber the grains of sand!"
—Psalm 139:17-18

What can you do to learn to recognize the way God speaks to you?

 What can you do to communicate your thoughts to God?

 According to James 1:17, what can you expect from God, your Father? What does this mean to you?

 Do you find it easy or hard to trust God? Explain your answer.

 Why do you think God may ask you to surrender something?

 Why do you think God wants to give you good gifts?

 How does God give you these gifts?

create your life

God asks you,
"What do you want from me?"

You ask God,
"What do you want from me?"

Write your answers to the questions on this page.
Then get a piece of blank paper and a pen or
pencil from your leader and write a prayer to
God, sharing your heart about what you are
surrendering and why.

Take about 10 minutes.

What does exchanging gifts with God make you think of?

"'Exchanging' gifts with God...what an appropriate word for such a concept. It constantly amazes me how wonderfully creative God was to give each and every one of us our own special abilities, gifts, and talents; no two are alike. He created each and every one of you for a specific purpose and has already given you the tools to live out the unique purpose he has for you. When a woman is earnestly seeking the Lord and using the gifts that he has given her to please him, she is treating him to the best she has to offer, which truly is a gift to him. The exchanging of gifts goes like this: 'Daughter, I love you and have a wonderful plan for you. Out of this deep love, I give to you the gifts that I know you will glorify me with.' To this, a young woman of God would say, 'Lord, I love you, and I want to praise and honor you with these gifts so that I can be drawn closer and closer to your heart and your vision for my life.'"

—Diana, a Pearl from Puerto Rico

"Giving over the control of my life, really letting go, and letting him be in charge. I am learning to be transparent, to be honest about my battles, to take off facades and masks in the atmosphere of genuine friends who live Christianity and who God gave me to share things in confidence and safety."

—Maleah, a Pearl from Florida

Express Yourself

Have one person read this aloud:

Ephesians 3:20 says, "Now all glory to God, who is able, through his mighty power at work within us, to accomplish infinitely more than we might ask or think." God can do more in our lives than we could even imagine possible. But we have to be willing to let him work in our lives. This takes that gift of surrender.

As you get ready to express yourself on your creative page, think of a symbol to represent what you are offering to God. If you're ready to do so, include what you wrote on your note to God. You're also going to put that note into a gift box and set that aside as a symbol of your gift of surrender.

Take one of the pretty gift boxes and pieces of pink ribbon from your leader. Fold the paper that you wrote on during the "Create Your Life" activity, and place this inside your box. Tie it shut with ribbon, and curl the ends of the ribbon. Write your name on the bottom of your box so it doesn't get mixed up with someone else's.

Then, on the blank page in this section, illustrate what you are surrendering to God as a gift to him. Use anything that will help you picture what your gift looks like. You may want to use one of the verses from the "Reflections" page in your expression.

When you are done, write a short prayer, and date your page.

Questions to ponder as you work on your creative page:

Rejoice. What do I have to be thankful for?

Rebuild. How do I struggle with this?

Renew. Look at my life through the eyes of truth. What does the Bible say?

Restore. What is God asking of me to work on? What am I asking of God to do in me?

Refine. What have I learned from this? How will I adjust my life to God's truth?

Remember. What symbol or image will help me remember this?

Role Models. Who shines this truth for me? How?

Ripple. Who can I shine for? How?

Sharing Life

Gather in groups of three or four to share the gift pages you have created. Remember to make this a time of encouragement.

Take at least 10 minutes to share.

Wrap It Up

Have everyone gather together and stand in a circle, placing the gift boxes at their feet, and hold hands. Have one person read "A Closing Reflection" aloud, considering these words adapted from Scripture as encouragement from God. If you are the leader, share your own closing thoughts so your group time is more personal. Close your time in prayer.

If you're at the beach, have everyone sit down in a row along the water's edge and put their boxes in front of them in the sand. Then as one person reads the closing thoughts, the other members of the group will close their eyes as they listen.

A Closing Reflection

Oh, my girls...thank you. For learning to trust me with your hearts. The plans I have for you are for good. I promise. Plans to give you a hope and a future. I want you to know...I have heard your prayers. I know your names, your thoughts, your dreams. I know your struggles, obstacles, defeats. I know you are courageous, loving, determined. Carry on, my girls; keep looking up.

When you search for me, you will find me. You will discover I'm already with you, ready to be a light for your path, leading you to live out your full potential. And remember, when you come to a season of surrender, I am thinking above and beyond all the ways you can ever guess or imagine. Letting go allows for a season of creation where I can make all things new. You can trust me. I am Faithful and True.

Make a Splash!

Play Jessica McLean's song "Designed to Dream."

my wave

"A spiritual gift is given to each of us so we can help each other."
—1 Corinthians 12:7

"If my fire is not large it is yet real, and there may be those who can light their candle at its flame."
—A.W. Tozer

"Make a careful exploration of who you are and the work you have been given, and then sink yourself into that. Don't be impressed with yourself. Don't compare yourself with others. Each of you must take responsibility for doing the creative best you can with your own life."
—Galatians 6:4-5

"Don't look down at the darkness of the disappearing sun, but look up to the color God can paint with your life!"
—Christina DiMari

"The Lord says, 'I will guide you along the best pathway for your life. I will advise you and watch over you.'"
—Psalm 32:8

"God can do anything, you know—far more than you could ever imagine or guess or request in your wildest dreams! He does it not by pushing us around but by working within us, his Spirit deeply and gently within us."
—Ephesians 3:20

This session draws *You're Designed to Shine!* to a close with encouragement to look forward and follow the plan God has set in motion for each person. You and your friends can reflect on what you've learned through this shared experience and consider new ways God might be encouraging you all to step out in faith.

➤ Supplies and Prep

If you're leading this session, you'll need to gather art supplies, such as old magazines, markers, pens, colored pencils, scissors, and glue sticks, and place these in a central location.

Let's Get Started!

Open your time together with a brief prayer. Then have one person from your group read this aloud:

Wherever you've come from, wherever you find yourself right now, whatever your future holds...you are designed to shine! God has designed you to shine. It doesn't matter your age, your work, or your experience, God has designed you to be unique, like no one else here, and he has a plan for you. Our adventure together has been amazing, and now it's time to ride the ultimate wave in life!

The Bible, in 1 Corinthians 12, says that God has given a gift to each of us, and we're to use this gift to help others. By doing this, we bring honor to God. Today we're going to explore the gifts God has in store for us and consider how we can use these to help others.

Have someone read "Sharing Stories" aloud.

Discover how Christina's been riding the wave of God's dream for her life and how you too can become part of the dream of shining for girls and women in your own community by reading her memoir, *Ocean Star.* Visit her website at www.oceanstargifts.com.

Sharing Stories

I stood alone, barefoot on the cool sand that glistened in the moonlight, my eyes fixed on the dolphin pod playing in the wave. The last remnants of color faded from the horizon, and the nighttime sky blazed with zillions of glowing stars. My hair blew in the salty, wet wind as I ambled in the calm, shallow water. I tilted my head back, fixing my attention upon the stars' shimmering light gleaming in the sky.

"Thank you, God," I whispered. "Your Spirit hovers over the water, and it is here that you have shown me how to find my way home. You are the one I hear when I listen to the quiet shifts of the changing tide. You are the one I recognize through the symbols of the sea. When the thrashing waves threatened to take me down, you showed me how to find my Rock and hold on tight. You are the Great Comforter and Healer. Through the powerful and gentle work of your Living Water, you have healed the broken pieces of my star and filled me with your light so I can shine for others."

In my mind's eye, I imagined thousands and thousands of girls from all over the world coming to the water to be encouraged. A question came to my mind: **If you could say something to these girls, what would you say?**

I reached for my bag and pulled out a dried starfish. Using the leg of the ocean star, I knelt down to write what came to my mind: **Believe, Dream, You matter, Friendship, Look up, Discover Pearls, God is with you, Don't give up, Celebrate, Go the distance, Love never fails, Forgive, Let go, Love, Create, Be yourself, Shine bright, Ride the wave of God's dream for your life!**

I continued writing until the shoreline was covered with words.

Then I stood and talked to God about all my words. It came to me. His Words are gifts to me. My words can be gifts to him. So I prayed that he would take my words and bring them into the lives of women all over the world who need encouragement.

The dolphin pod continued to play in the roll wave close to shore, while the coming tide covered my words and took them out to sea.

Encouragement

Have someone read this aloud:

Christina wanted to share some personal words of encouragement with us all at this time. I'm going to read this message from her to you.

Riding the wave of God's dream for your life is not found as much by figuring things out in your head or following a five-step plan as it is by feeling the rhythm of the water. A seasoned surfer can feel a set of waves coming long before they actually see them. That's why I start off this study with thinking about your dreams, to help you get into the deep inner longings of your heart.

The heart is central. It is where Christ dwells. It is where the dreams God has for your life have been deposited. It is where the rivers of living water flow. It is where creative expression is released.

It is a wonderful thing to have a dream. When you ride the wave of God's dream for your life, you are using the gifts and dreams inside of you to use your life in creative ways to shine the love of Christ to others. There is really nothing more rewarding than this. And you can start now. No matter your age. Really.

In the beginning of this adventure, you explored some of your dreams; you've learned the importance of traveling with a supportive pod, discovering Pearls for your journey, and deepening your relationship with God. All of this is leading up to this chapter, where you realize that your uniqueness and originality are all part of God's design for your life. Let God flow his love through you!

What's your wave? The Bible says that God has given each of us different spiritual gifts—strengths that we should use to help others. In 1 Corinthians 12, we're given sort of a visual picture of what this is like—a body. What do you think is the most important body part and the least important body part?

Take a few minutes to discuss this question in small groups. After a few minutes, have groups share their thoughts with everyone.

Then have one person read aloud:

You can see that we can't really say one part is more important than another. Without many of our body parts, we'd die. Without a lot of them, we'd be miserable. Every part is important; even the parts that don't *seem* important really do matter. It's the same with us and the abilities and strengths God has given us. We're all good at different things, and when we all work together, we make a complete body, or team, that gets everything done and shines brightly, reflecting the love of Christ.

We're going to use a symbol from the ocean—a wave—to help us think about using our special abilities to shine brightly. When someone is riding a wave, she's using every part of her body to do something amazing. Everything is working together. When we use our gifts and work together with others, it's like riding that exciting wave!

Knowing Jesus

Do you know what it means to be a Christian? If you are the leader, take time now to be sure each person in your group knows the simple message of God's love, his gift of Jesus and his death and resurrection, and the grace we receive when we accept God's gift. If you're not sure how to do this, you'll find a simple plan outlined on pages 91 and 92.

reflections

Read the questions here, and take time to write your thoughts. You'll have the opportunity to share your thoughts later, but now it's time for personal reflection. Take about 20 minutes for this time of reflection.

What are your strengths? Name at least five.

Beside each of the strengths you listed above, write a way God could use that to help someone else, through your actions.

What makes you feel alive and excited or gives you a rush of adrenaline? If you see this fitting within God's boundaries for your life, this could be the way God shines through your life to be a light for others.

What would you choose to do to help someone today?

What are your favorite topics to study? How could your interest or knowledge in these areas help someone?

How are you riding the wave of God's dream for your life?

"I have never felt that God's dream for me was a sincerely spectacular one. No, God's dream for me is so very practical. Become like him. Adopt his characteristics. Serve wholeheartedly. Love despite rejection. Look at the world through his eyes, always with eternity in mind."

—Maddie, a Pearl from London

What's something you love to do and that helps others?

 God designed you for a one-of-a-kind wave to ride. Write about a time in the past when you felt you rode a wave God brought your way. What about in the present? How about something you are hoping for the future?

How can you stay authentic to who God wants you to be?

Be ready when the waves of opportunity come because, believe me, as you apply the lessons we've been learning together, the waves are coming!

What's your favorite way to shine God's love?

"Even just a smile can give him glory, or a tear of compassion in your concern for others. Make your every day an expression of his love! And if you blow it? His mercies are new every morning!"
— Bethany Hamilton, shark attack survivor and a Pearl from Hawaii

"I started Surf 'n' Shine! I teach girls how to surf in the morning and how to live for God in the afternoon!"
— Melanie, a Pearl from Barbados

create your life

After answering the questions in the "Reflections" section, what are possible waves God has for you to ride? How can God use your special gifts and abilities to shine for him into the lives of others? Write your thoughts here, and draw a star beside those abilities you're most excited about.

You're an original!

You can do something in a way that no one else can. When you shine as the unique star that you are and use your dreams and life to shine God's love, help others, and make him known every day of your life, you're riding the ultimate wave of life!

Be authentic!

When you compare yourself to others, you will end up falling off of your wave and getting thrashed around in life's currents. Be you! When you stay true to who you are, you'll find the rhythm that God flows through you alone. That's when you'll get that rush of adrenaline pumping through your veins, calling out, "I was made to do this!"

Know your purpose!

Use your wave to shine God's love. You've been given this ride to make God known in a way that no one else can.

Stay pure!

Your purity demonstrates following God's best for your life and everything that goes with following his ways.

You're not alone!

God has gone before you. Wherever he leads you, whatever your future holds, he will always be with you. He said, "And be sure of this: I am with you always, even to the end of the age" (Matthew 28:20).

Express Yourself

Have one person read this aloud:

Galatians 6:4-5 says: "Make a careful exploration of who you are and the work you have been given, and then sink yourself into that. Don't be impressed with yourself. Don't compare yourself with others. Each of you must take responsibility for doing the creative best you can with your own life." This is the same verse we focused on during our first session together. It's likely this verse has taken on new meaning for each of us as we've had time to reflect on it over the past sessions.

On the following blank page, create a reminder of all you've learned on your journey through *You're Designed to Shine!* Use art, pictures, words, stickers, quotes, sand, ribbon, paper, fabric, or anything else that will help you remember what you've experienced and learned, that will help you pass this along to others coming up the road of life behind you. You may want to use one of the verses from the "Reflections" page in your expression.

When you're done, write a short prayer, and date your page.

Questions to ponder as you work on your creative page:

Rejoice. What do I have to be thankful for?

Rebuild. How do I struggle with this?

Renew. Look at my life through the eyes of truth. What does the Bible say?

Restore. What is God asking of me to work on? What am I asking of God to do in me?

Refine. What have I learned from this? How will I adjust my life to God's truth?

Remember. What symbol or image will help me remember this?

Role Models. Who shines this truth for me? How?

Ripple. Who can I shine for? How?

Sharing Life

Gather in groups of three or four to share the pages you created. Remember, this is a time to encourage each other and help others consider the possibilities that God might have ahead for them in life. Use this time to help a friend shine!

Take at least 10 minutes to share.

Wrap It Up

Gather together, and stand in a circle, holding hands. Have someone read aloud the "Closing Thoughts From Christina." These thoughts today are in the form of a prayer. If you are the leader, share your own closing thoughts so your group time is more personal. Close your time in prayer.

If you're at the beach, do this near the water's edge.

Closing Thoughts From Christina

Dear Father, I pray for all these amazing girls that you have created in your image. Make your presence known to each one right where they are.

Encourage them to continue dreaming big.

Woo them to your Living Water.

Invite them to find satisfaction in you alone.

Teach them to hold on to you, the Rock, when the waves of life toss them about.

Give them the gift of faith to follow you although they don't know where you're leading and discernment to travel with people who will support them.

Surprise them with pearls along the way who will shine for them in unexpected ways just when they need a bit of encouragement.

Instruct them in your ways.

Motivate them to surrender to you so you can create new things in their lives and allow room for their dreams to come true.

Surround each person here with your promises, your favor, and your love. Put your hand upon each one, and bless them. Pour all good and perfect gifts into their lives, and make them pure vessels so your gifts can flow out of them to others. Go before them, hem them in on each side, and may your glory be their rear guard. Protect them from all who would want to steal, kill, or destroy their dream and light.

Finish the work you started in each person on this journey. Let them know you are always with them, so when times are tough, they will still look up and carry on.

Shine your light through each one of these girls till the whole world can look up and find enough light to find their way home. Bring on the waves, dear God—these women are ready for the ride of their lives!

Make a Splash!

Play Jessica McLean's song "Designed to Dream."

notes for the leader

If you're leading *You're Designed to Shine!* this section will walk you through the basic steps of planning and will answer your questions.

Should I read *Ocean Star*?

Yes! This is certainly not a requirement, but it will be very helpful for you to understand the whole vision behind *You're Designed to Shine!* and understand Christina's faith journey. *Ocean Star* is available at Christian bookstores and at group.com.

What's the format for this study?

You're Designed to Shine! is an interactive and experiential study to encourage girls and women to become the shining stars God designed them to be. During each session, there will be times to share, to be creative, and to participate in individual and group activities. There are six sessions that can be done in a variety of formats. You can use this as a weekly study, as a weekend retreat, or in whatever way works best for your group.

What supplies do I need?

Each girl or woman will need her own copy of this book. You'll also need art supplies, such as old magazines, markers, pens, colored pencils, scissors, and glue sticks. These will be used in each session.

To make *You're Designed to Shine!* a truly shiny experience, we also recommend that you provide:

- 1 dried starfish per person (optional for session 1; used in session 2)

- 1 pearl or strand of freshwater pearls per person (used in session 4)

- 1 small gift box per person—choose a pretty gold-foil box if at all possible (used in session 5)

- pink curling ribbon (used in session 5)

- sheets of blank paper; pens or pencils (used in session 5)

Can I go through this experience by myself?

I would suggest trying to gather a group of friends to do it with you. If you can't find a group, yes, you can do it by yourself. I hope that when you're finished, you'll gather a group of younger girls and take them through it as their leader.

What age does this work best for?

This was originally created for girls in high school or college. But everyone wanted to bring younger sisters, and many, many women who were out of college (and well beyond!) wanted to join in. So we've included women of a much wider age span in *You're Designed to Shine!* One thing that should be stressed, though, is that girls come to this event to be encouraged, so do express that outlook to older women attending who may have become more cynical about life. Remind them they should come with a positive outlook to grow in their own journeys as well as to be a light for those younger than them.

How many can attend?

The size of your group is limited only by the size of your meeting area.

Do I have to be a speaker to lead this?

No, just comfortable enough to talk in a pretty laid-back fashion. This is all about sharing, not "speaking." The whole focus of this material is *not* on the abilities of the person leading it, but on the interactive experiences the girls will be participating in. In each session guide, Christina coaches you through what she normally says in each section.

Who leads the small groups?

The portions where girls are in smaller groups working together or discussing don't require much in the way of leadership—simply having someone there to make sure everyone gets a chance to talk and that the words shared are encouraging is enough.

I often try to get "Pearls" (girls or women who have gone through the material before) to come and help out. If you don't have that option, you can remind girls each week that one of them needs to make sure everyone gets a chance to talk, keep the group focused on what they're to do, and keep the conversation positive.

How are the small groups formed?

First, be sure that groups don't grow too large. A small group should never have more than six in it—there simply isn't enough time for everyone to share and complete the discussions if groups are larger than this.

Second, I suggest you assign the same girls to be together for at least two sessions so they can build relationships and trust with each other. Then you can have them form new groups for the next two, and again for the last two. Or you may choose to have everyone stay with their same groups for the entire experience so they really bond.

Do be tuned in to the group dynamics. If you feel someone may thrive or connect better in a different group, be flexible. Let the girls know up front they can chat with you about switching. If you have several groups, give each of them some sort of identity. I like to call them "pods" from different waters around the world. Let them decide where they want to be from. They could have a really good time deciding what island they're from and even have certain weeks where they dress from their location.

While you do want groups to bond, be careful not to let groups feel like exclusive cliques where some are left out and made to feel unwanted. This may be avoided if you assign members of groups instead of letting everyone choose their own groups.

How long does each session take?

Allow an hour and a half to two hours for each session.

How much preparation time is required?

These sessions are amazingly easy! Remember, they were designed to be easy enough that a girl of any age could lead them. Allow yourself enough time to read through each session entirely and to gather the supplies that you'll need. If you plan to decorate your area, want to bring snacks, or do other things that will add to your prep time, allow for that, as well. And don't forget to take time to pray for everyone who will be attending.

Where should we meet?

We like to do our settings outside as much as possible. Depending on where you live, consider meeting on the beach, near a lake, stream, river, or pond, in your backyard, or at a nearby park.

However, you can certainly meet inside, as well. A home provides a cozy setting for a smaller group, or you can use a church, community center, or even a school gym if you need to.

When meeting indoors, you can have girls sit with their groups on blankets on the floor, or you can have them sit in chairs around tables. Be sure to consider other factors that make everyone comfortable, such as having enough space, having adequate lighting, good smells, and so on. You might also want to provide snacks—at least something to drink.

If you're meeting outside, it's a good idea to have a backup location in case of bad weather. If you are on a beach or public area, get a permit, if necessary—check with local authorities to see if you need one! Again, sitting on blankets is easy for outdoors and makes everyone more comfortable. Bottled water is good for outside events, with very simple snacks such as cookies or crackers.

Do I need to decorate?

If you're meeting outdoors, there won't be much decorating to do. Just make sure you have blankets or sheets for groups to sit on.

If you need to meet indoors, it's more fun if you set the tone with some decorations. You can do this yourself, or gather a Design Team and let them have fun with it! Some easy ideas:

- Keep all color choices blue, white, sand, and green...with an occasional punch of coral for spunk.

- Play sounds of waves and other ocean sounds, or choose upbeat beach or island tunes.

- Use sand and shells for centerpieces or other spot decorations.

    - Put all of the art supplies on a table, along with shells and sand.

Can I do *You're Designed to Shine!* as a retreat?

Sure! If you decide to do this as a retreat or large event, you'll need to choose a pod of helpers who won't bail on you and leave you to do it all yourself! It makes it more fun this way, too, and usually ends up being way more creative with more brains in the mix. You also will have someone to rejoice with when the event is over as you see the girls impacted on their journey.

Have people on your team take charge of these areas:

- prayer
- publicity
- location logistics
- decorating
- hospitality and registration
- food
- sound system
- follow-up
- photography
- security (If you have a gathering of girls, it's a good idea to have protectors around, especially near entrances, exits, and restrooms.)

How do I help someone else make the decision to become a Christian?

It's likely that some who participate in this study do not know Jesus yet and may have never even heard that God sent his Son, Jesus, to die for our sins because he loves us.

If you sense that someone might like to know more about what it means to follow Jesus and become a Christian, here is a very simple explanation:

God loves us so much that he sent his Son, Jesus, to die on the cross for us. Jesus died and came back to life so we could be forgiven for all the wrong things we do—sin. Jesus wants to be our friend and have an everlasting relationship with us. If we ask him to, he'll forgive our sins—those wrong things we've done—and fill our lives with his love. Jesus will always be with us and will help us make the right choices. And if we believe in Jesus and ask him to forgive us, someday we'll live with him in heaven forever.

You may want to pray with the girl or woman, helping her to invite Jesus into her life. You may also want to read these Scripture passages from a Bible.

- John 3:16
- Romans 5:8-11
- Romans 6:23
- Ephesians 2:4-8

And remember, this is a reason to celebrate! Encourage her to share her decision to follow Jesus with others!

Enjoy!

I know you are going to have an amazing time on this adventure! I pray that God will give you love, discernment, and joy as you lead girls and women deeper into understanding how each one is designed by God to shine his love in this world.

Thanks for being willing to be a Pearl!

Christina
DiMari*

"Those who are wise will shine like the brightness of the heavens, and those who lead many to righteousness, like the stars for ever and ever."

—Daniel 12:3

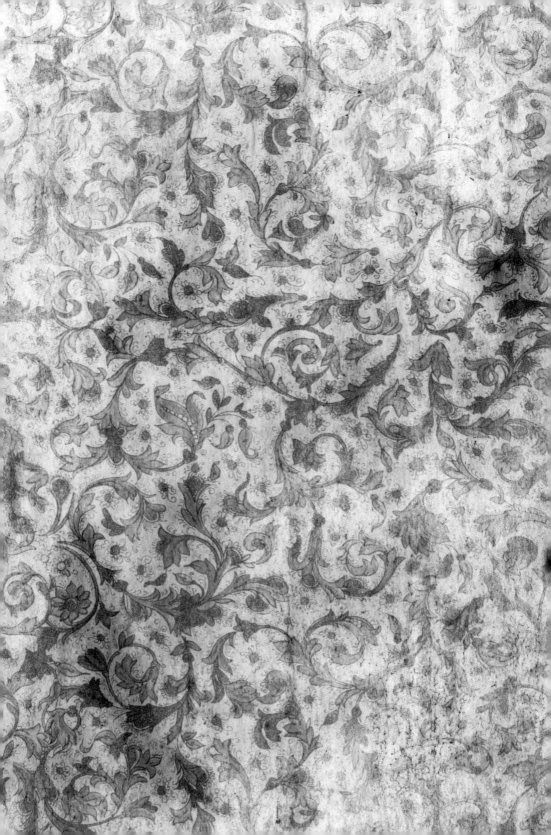